MY BOOK OF FIRST 1000 WORDS

This book belongs to

....

Alphabets

Aa Apple

Bb Balloon

Cc Cat

Dd Doll

Ee Eagle

Ff Flowers

Gg
Giraffe

Hh
House

Ii

Ice

Jj
Juice

Kk
Kettle

Ll
Ladybug

Alphabets

Mm

Mango

Nn

Noodles

Oo

Orange

Pp

Puppy

Qq

Question

Rr

Rabbit

Ss
Shoes

Tt
Tiger

Uu
Utensils

Vv
Volcano

Ww
Walnut

Xx
Xylophone

Yy
Yolk

Zz
Zebra

Numbers

1  One	2  Two
3  Three	4  Four
5  Five	6   Six
7  Seven	8  Eight
9  Nine	10  Ten

 Eleven	 Twelve
 Thirteen	 Fourteen
  Fifteen	 Sixteen
Seventeen	Eighteen
Nineteen	 Twenty

Colours

Yellow   **Sunflower**

Green   **Cabbage**

Blue   **Butterfly**

Orange   **Traffic Cone**

Pink   **Purse**

Red   **Rose**

Brown   **Chocolate**   **Magenta**   **Ice Candy**

Black   **Crow**   **Golden**   **Gold Ring**

Grey   **Elephant**   **Purple**   **Sapphire**

Shapes

Star	Starfish	Christmas Star

Heart	Candy	Leaf

Diamond	Kite	Spinning Top

Crescent	Moon	Banana

Cone	Ice Cream Cone	Birthday Cap

Oval	**Mirror**	**Egg**

Triangle	**Pizza Slice**	**Sandwich**

Rectangle	**Book**	**Television**

Square	**Carrom Board**	**Dice**

Circle	**Football**	**Cookies**

Opposites

Old	New	Hot	Cold
Sit	Stand	Full	Empty
Fast	Slow	Heavy	Light
Solid	Liquid	Dirty	Clean

	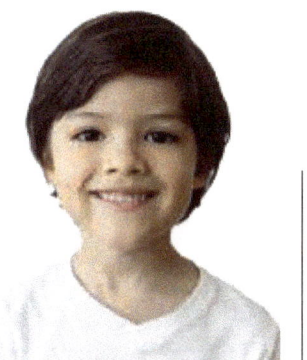		
Sad	**Happy**	**Sweet**	**Sour**

Big	**Small**	**Outside**	**Inside**

Up	**Down**	**Open**	**Close**

Hard	**Soft**	**Front**	**Back**

Food

Butter

Milk

Ice Cream

Hotdog

Burger

Cookies

Pizza

Sandwich

Yogurt

Fish

Cheese

Muffin

Fruit Salad

Chocolate

Egg

Shrimp

Cake

Food

Honey

Salad

Chicken

Soup

Potato Finger

Cornflakes

Popcorn

Fruits

Avocado

Dragon Fruit

Muskmelon

Blueberry

Blackberry

Custard Apple

Coconut

Java Plum

Vegetables

Carrot

Beetroot

Onion

Bitter Gourd

Cauliflower

Lady Finger

Pumpkin

Turnip

People at Work

Astronaut

Scientist

Pilot

Photographer

Doctor

Baker

Police Officer

Farmer

Nurse

Electrician

Gardener

Transport

Bus

Lorry

Car

Scooter

Tandem

Golf Cart

Unicycle

Digger

Motorcycle

Skateboard

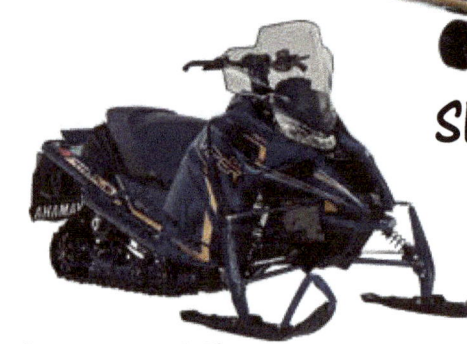
Snowmobile

Food Wagon

Garbage Truck

Cycle

Caravan

Tow Truck

Oil Tanker

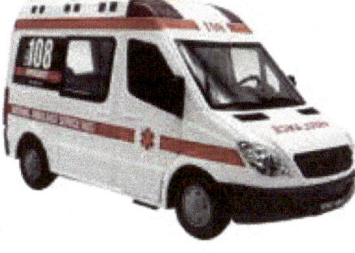

Ambulance

Go Cart

Van

Tractor

Truck

Fire Truck

Taxi

Pet & Farm Animals

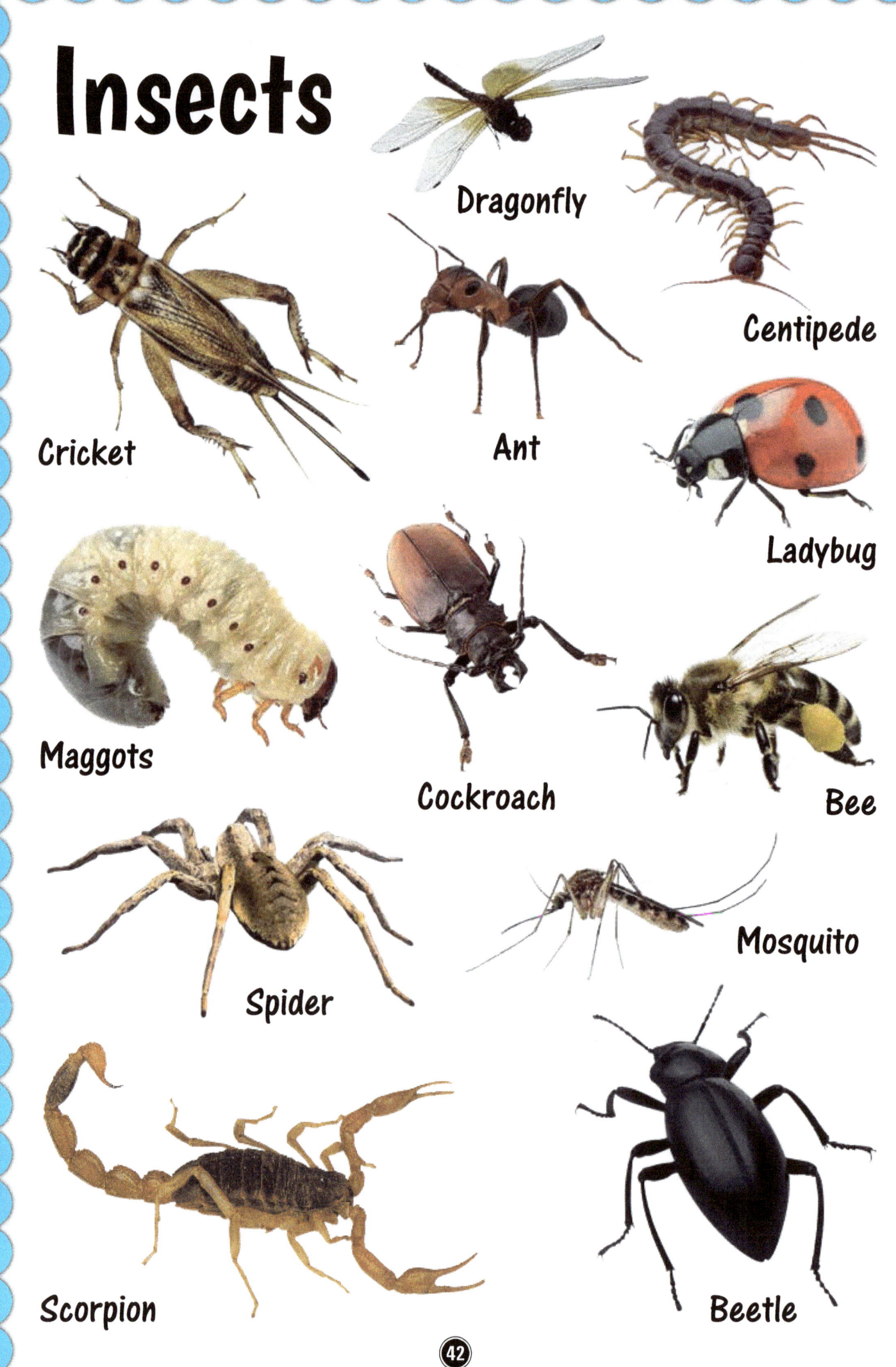

My Body

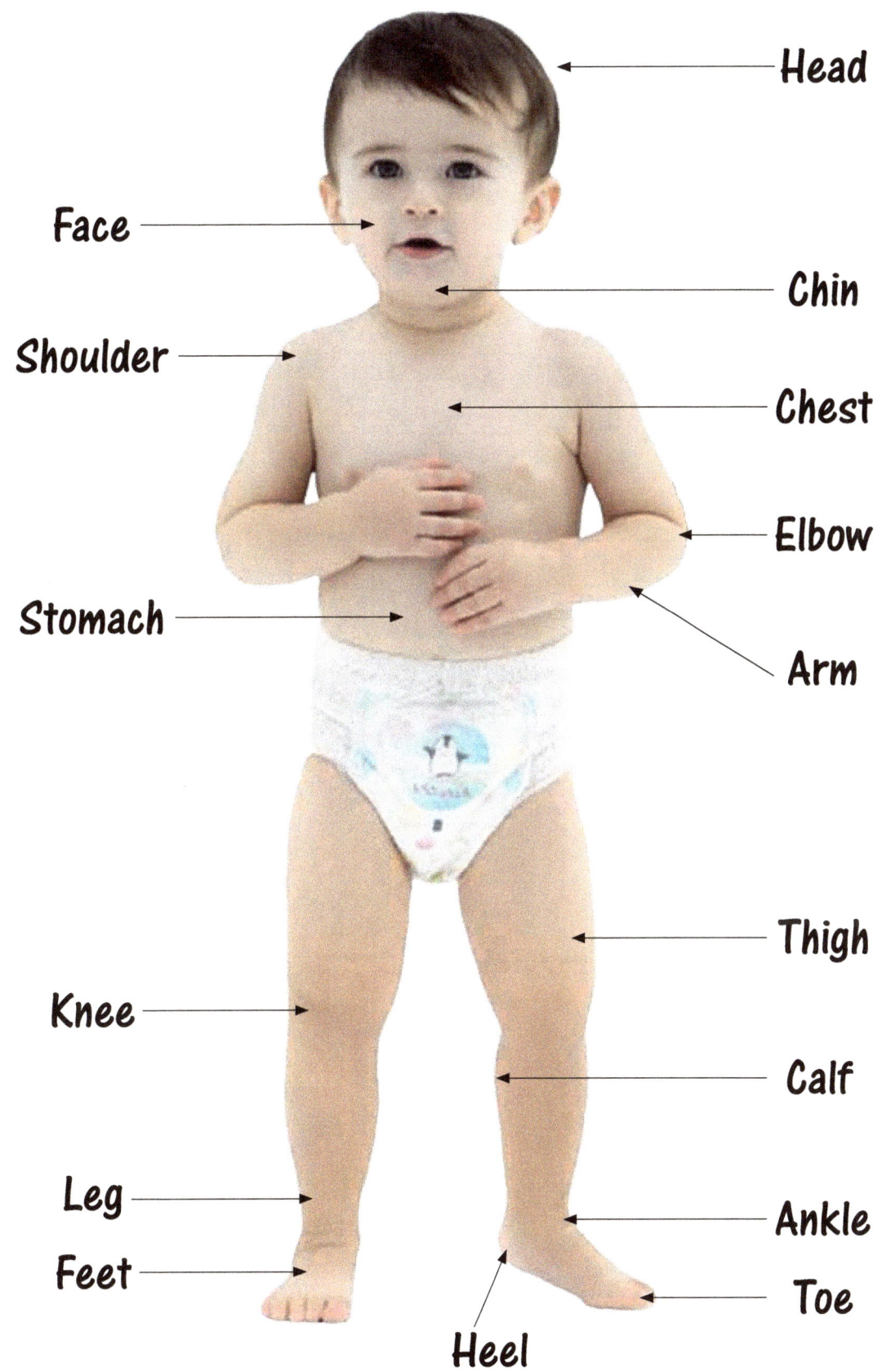

My Face

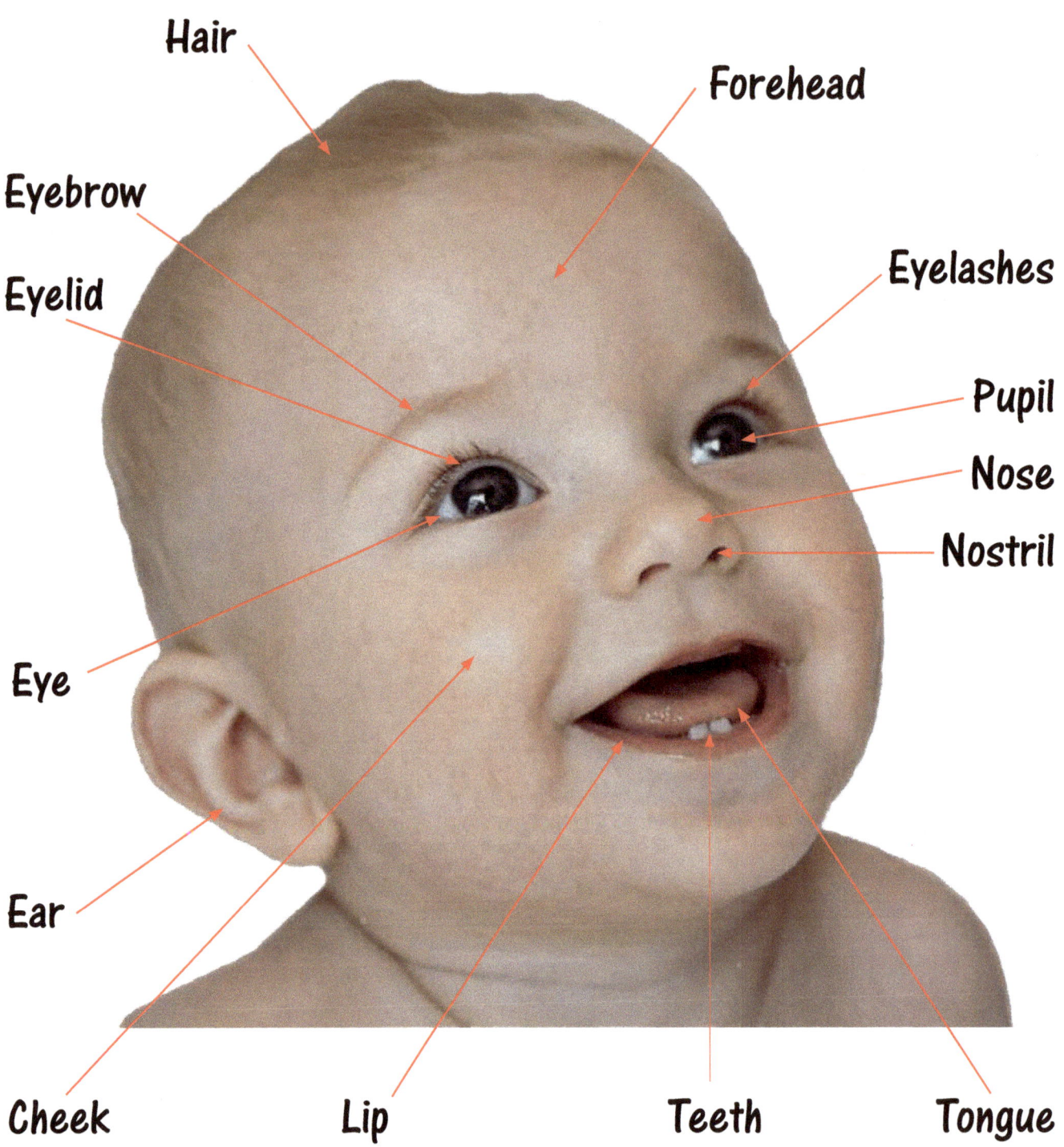

My Hands

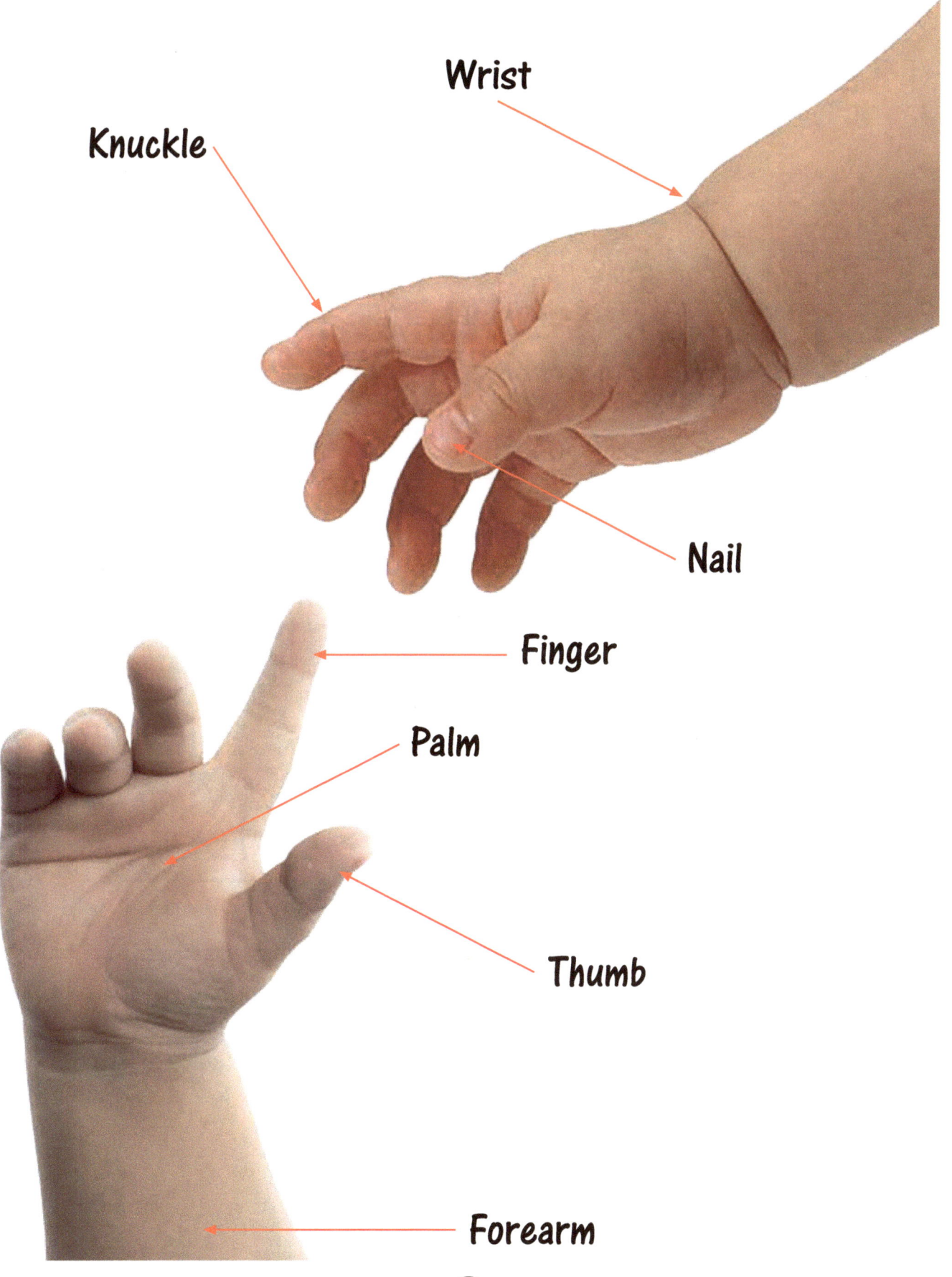

Baby Faces

Laughing

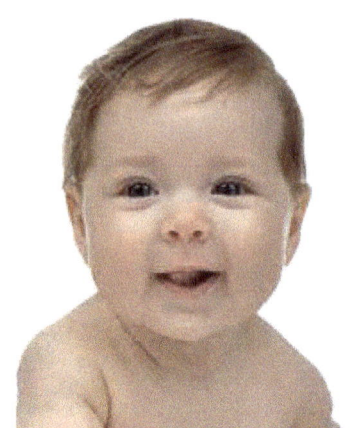
Smiling

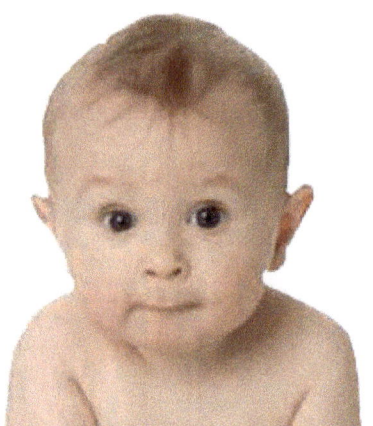
Surprised

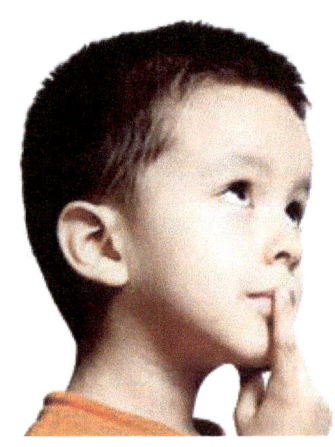
Thinking

Yawning

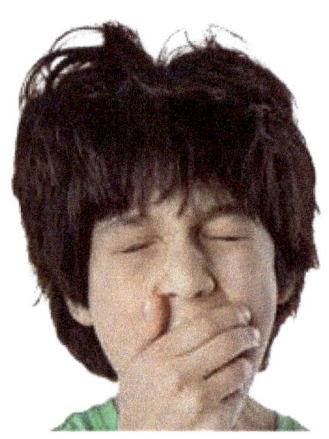
Sleepy

Excited

Crying

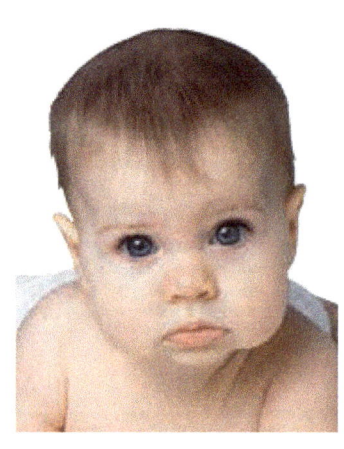
Sad

My Senses

Toys

Superman

Ring Donut

Rubik's Cube

Truck

Smart Phone

Rocket

Teddy

Robot

Hulk

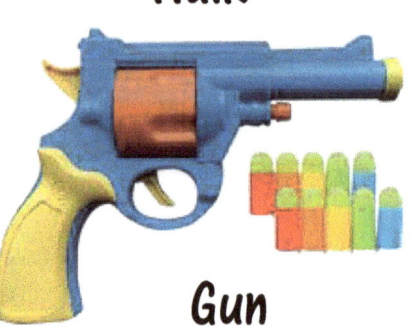
Gun

Top

Toy Cycle

Remote Car

Skipping Rope

Spin Rattle

Spiderman

Labyrinth

Ball

Slide Car

Camera

School Bus

Toys

Car

Police Bike

Blocks

Kitchen Set

Doll

Finger Puppets

Slider

Dinosaur

Aeroplane

Jeep

Piano

Bike

Drum

Activity Toy

Fire Truck

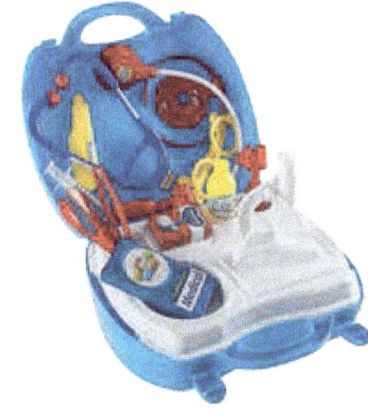
Doctor Set

Phone

Jumping Castle

Trolley

Rattle

Activity Toy

Duck

Police Car

Rocking Horse

Toy Train

Objects Around the Baby

Rattle

High Chair

Pacifier

Diaper

Romper

Bathtub

Crib

Booties

Oil

Objects Around the Baby

In the Living Room

Sofa

Clock

Flowerpot

Air Conditioner

Chair

Hanging Light

Curtain

Carpet

Television

Phone

Fireplace

Center Table

In the Bedroom

Bed

Quilt

Table Lamp

Pillow

Drawer

Clock

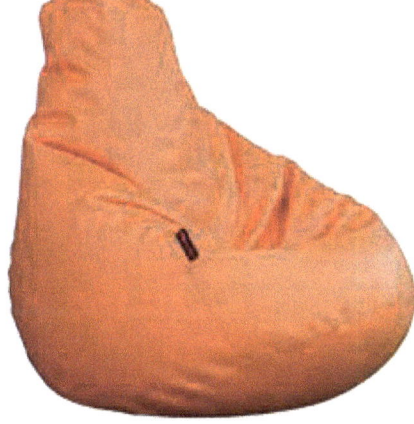
Bean Bag

Doormat

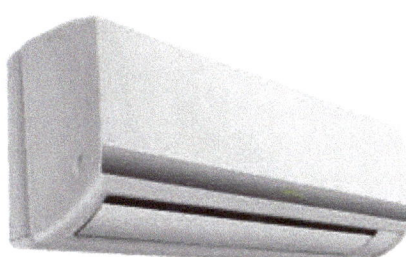
Air Conditioner

Fan

Dressing Table

Wardrobe

In the Bathroom

Loofah

Washbasin

Hair Dryer

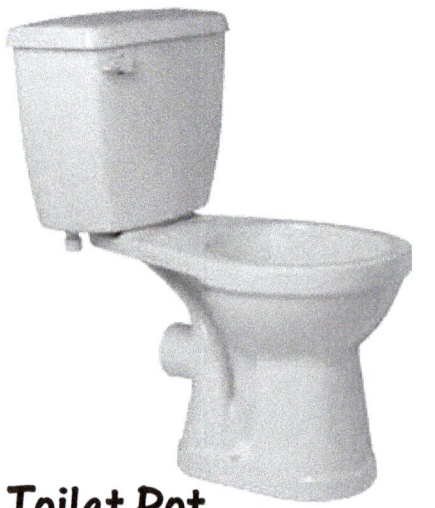
Toilet Pot

Washing Powder

Mouth Freshener

Laundry Hamper

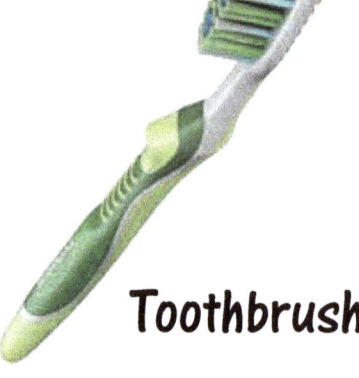
Toothbrush

Mug

Soap Dish

Bucket

Sponge

Soap

Hair Brush

Hair Oil

Shampoo

Tissue Paper

Exhaust Fan

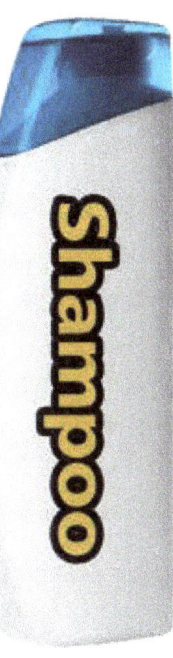
Toothpaste

Towel

Bathbrush

Mirror

Washing Machine

Shower

Toilet Paper

Blinds

Kitchen Appliances

Refrigerator

Whisk

Chimney

Apron

Cup & Saucer

Cooking Pan

Pressure Cooker

Mixer Grinder

Coffee Machine

Washbasin

Toaster

Action Words

Drinking

Dancing

Praying

Hiding

Jumping

Bending

Playing

Eating

Feeling Surprised

Kicking

Running

Crawling

Crying

Feeling Angry

Talking

Washing

Sweeping

Musical Instruments

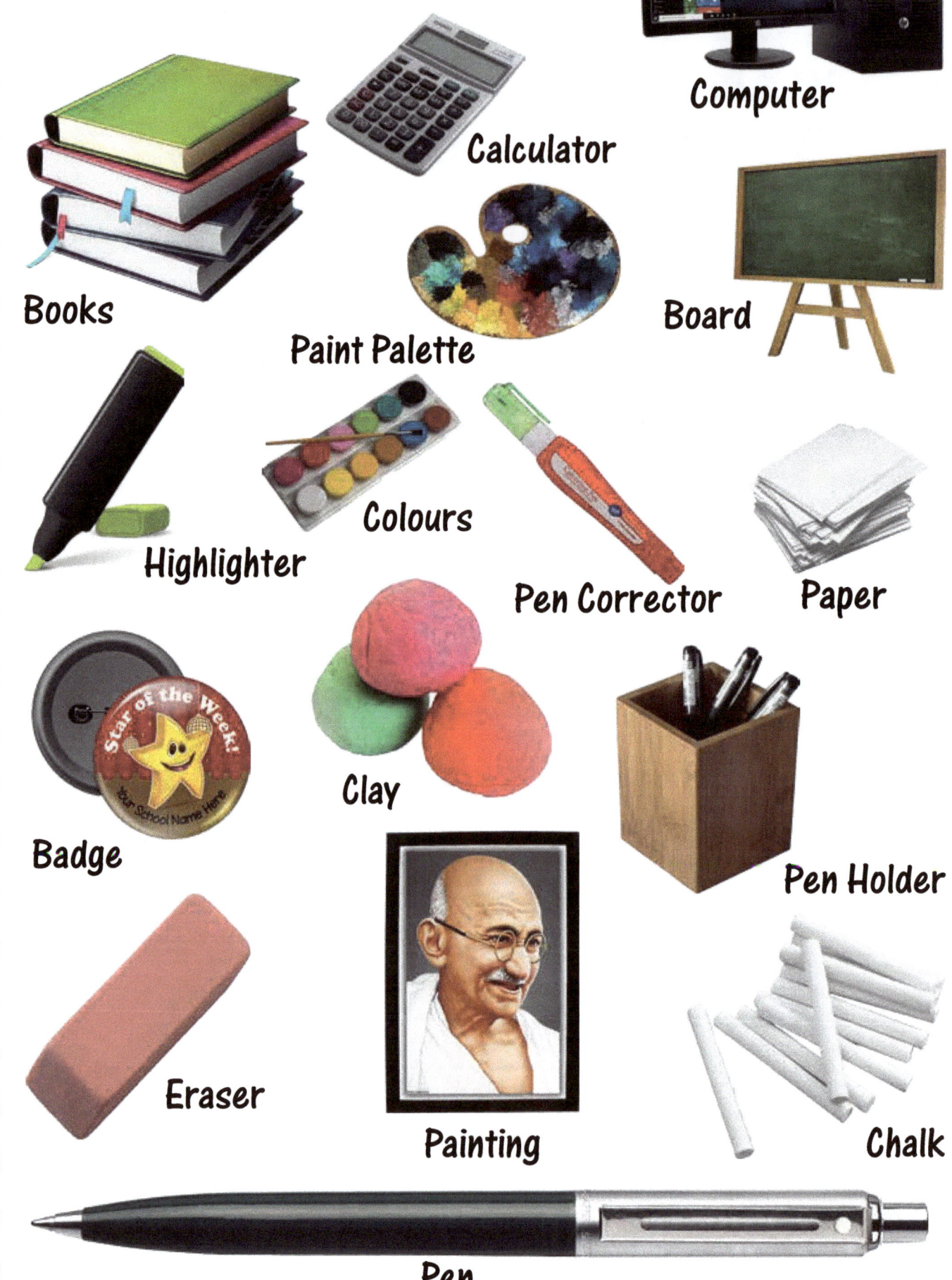

Clothes

Shirt

Gloves

Sweater

Pajamas

Scarf

Shorts

Woollen Cap

Skirt

Shawl

Frock

Gown

Long Coat

Accessories

Necklace

Sunglasses

Key Chain

Watch

Bow Tie

Wallet

Belt

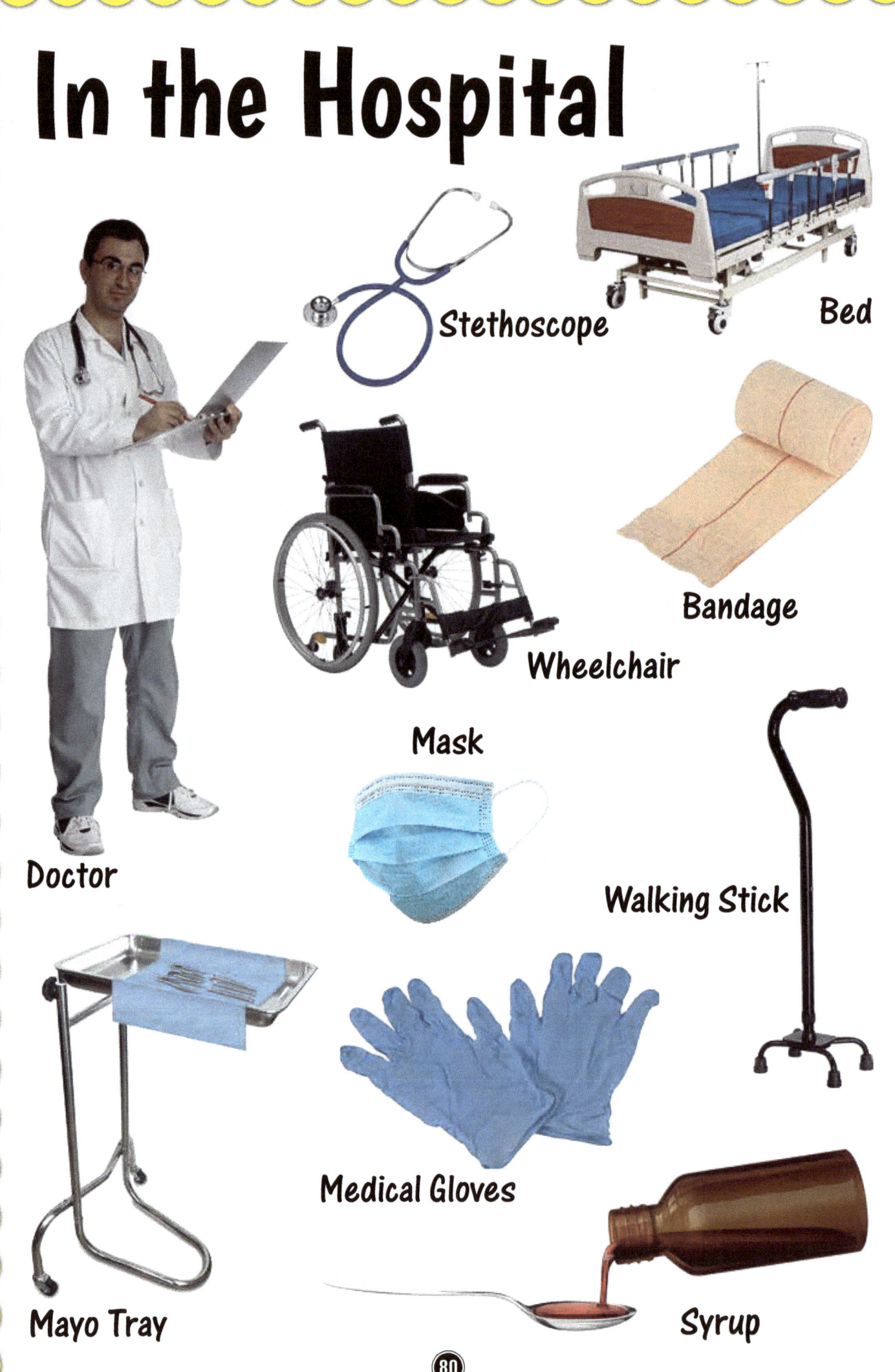

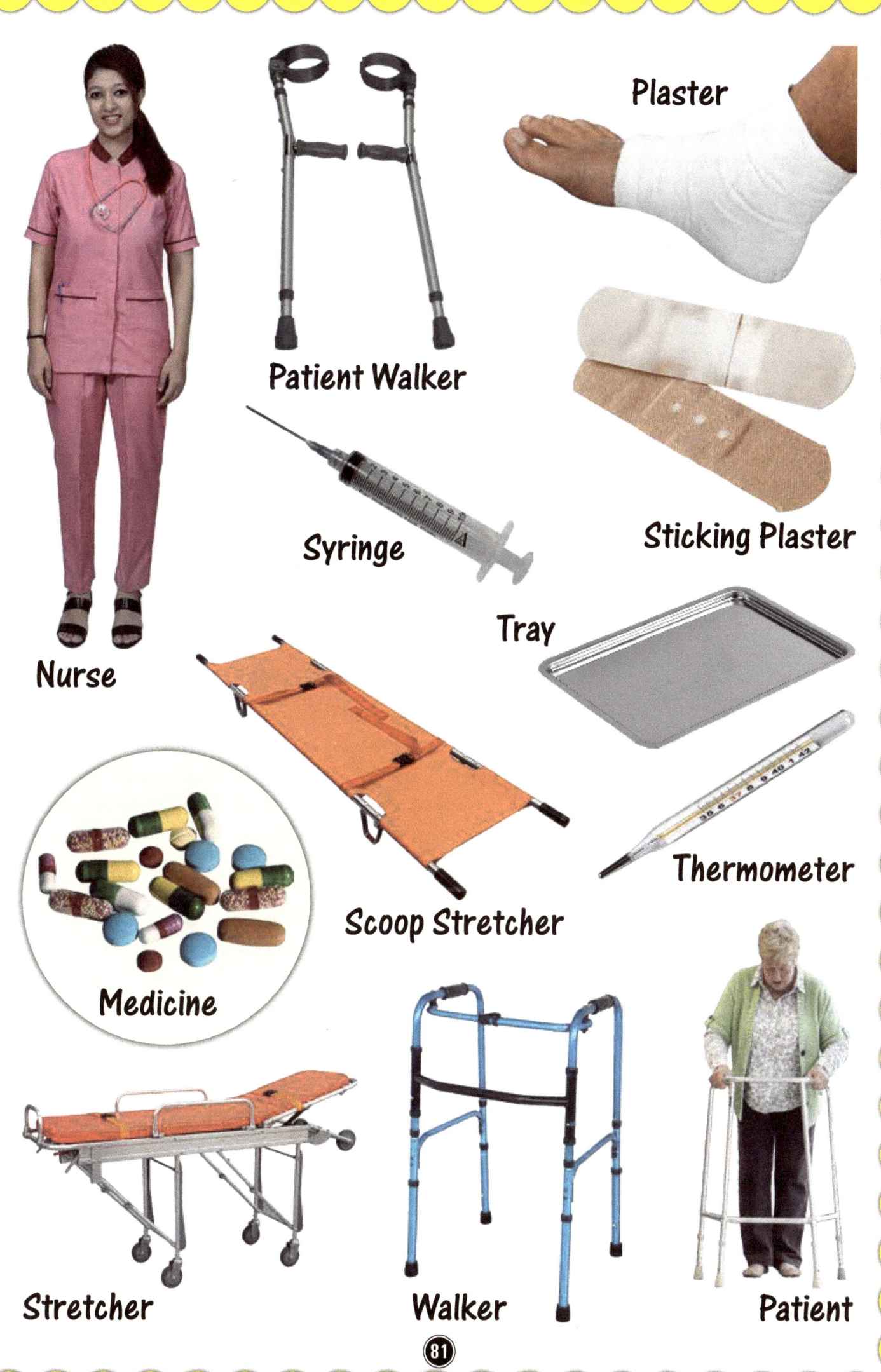

In the Park

Push Chair

Merry-Go-Round

Tree

Bench

Sandpit

Play House

See Saw

Fountain

Lamp Post

Picnic Basket

Statue

Path

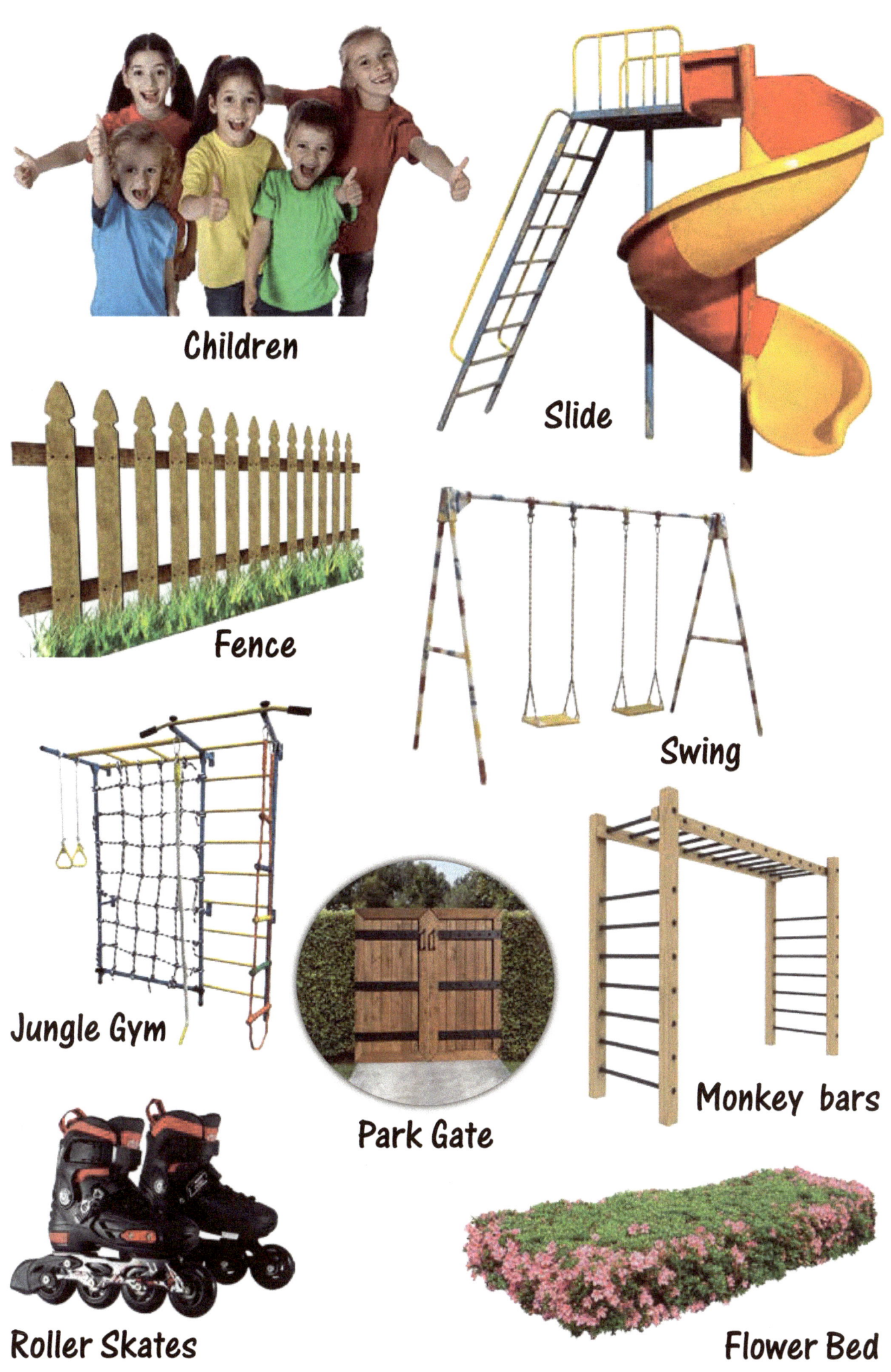

At the Circus

Circus Tent

Trapeze

Rope Trapeze

Cyr Wheel

Static Trapeze

Clown

Words' List

A

Accessories	78
Accordion	68
Acrobatics	87
Action Words	62
Activity Toy	51
Aeroplane	30, 50
Air Conditioner	56, 57
Alphabets	2
Ambulance	29
Anger	65
Ankle	43
Ant	42
Apple Gourd	24
Apple	2, 18
Apron	60
Archery	74
Architect	27
Arm	43
Asparagus	23
Aster	67
Astronaut	26
Auto Rikshaw	31
Avocado	20

B

Baby Animals	38
Baby Faces	46
Baby Objects	52
Baby Platypus	39
Back	13
Backpack	82
Badge	72
Bag	79
Bagpipe	71
Baker	26
Ball	49
Balloon	2
Banana	10, 18
Bandage	80
Bangles	79
Banjo	70
Baseball	75
Basketball	74
Bass Drum	70
Bat	33
Bathbrush	59
Bathroom	58
Bathtub	52
Bean Bag	57
Bear Cub	38
Bear	37
Bed	57, 80
Bedroom	57
Bee	42
Beetle	42
Beetroot	22
Belt	78
Bench	84
Bending	62
Bib	54
Big	13
Bike	50
Binoculars	82
Birds House	88
Birds	32
Birthday Cap	10
Bitter Gourd	22
Black Olives	21
Black	9
Blackberry	20
Blanket	55
Blazer	77
Blimp	30
Blinds	59
Blocks	50
Blue	8
Bluebell	67
Blueberry	20
Boar	37
Board	72
Boat	31
Bongo Drum	68
Book	11
Books	72
Booties	52
Bottle	53
Bottle Gourd	24
Bouncer	54
Bow Tie	78
Bowl	54
Boxing	75
Bracelet	79
Bread	17
Broccoli	25
Brown	9
Brush	73
Bucket	58
Buffalo	34
Bull	35
Burger	14
Bus	28
Butter	14
Buttercup	67
Butterfly	8

C

Cabbage	8, 24
Cable Car	30
Cake	15
Calculator	72
Calf	39, 43
Camera	49, 83
Camp	82
Camping	82
Candy	10
Canna	67
Cap	53
Capsicum	23
Car Seat	54
Car	28, 50
Caravan	29
Cardigan	77
Cargo Ship	30
Carnation	67
Carpenter	27
Carpet	56
Carrom Board	11
Carrier	55

Carrot	22	Colt	38	Diamond	10
Cat	2, 34	Comb	53	Diaper	52
Catching	64	Compass	83	Dice	11
Caterpillar	39	Computer	72	Digger	28
Catfish	41	Cone	10	Dinosaur	50
Cauliflower	22	Construction Worker	27	Dirty	12
Celery	23	Cookies	11, 14	Dish Washer	61
Center Table	56	Cooking Pan	60	Doctor Set	51
Centipede	42	Cooking Pot	61	Doctor	26, 80
Chair	56	Coral	41	Dog	34
Chalk	72	Coriander	25	Doll	2, 50
Cheek	44	Cornflakes	16	Dolphin	41
Cheese	15	Cow	35	Donkey	35
Cheetah	36	Crab	41	Doormat	57
Chef	27	Crane	32	Doughnut	17
Cherry	18	Crawl	65	Dove	32
Chest	43	Crescent	10	Down	13
Chick	34, 39	Crib	52	Dragonfish	41
Chicken	16	Cricket	42, 75	Dragon Fruit	20
Children	85	Crocodile	36	Dragonfly	42
Chimney	60	Crow	9, 33	Drawer	57
Chimpanzee	36	Cry	65	Dressing Table	57
Chin	43	Crying	46	Drinking	62
Chocolate	9, 15	Cucumber	24	Drum Set	68
Chopping Board	61	Cup & Saucer	60	Drum	50
Christmas Star	10	Curtain	56	Drumstick	25
Circle	11	Custard Apple	20	Duck	32, 34, 51
Circus Tent	86	Cut	64	Duckling	38
Circus	86	Cutlery	61	Dustbin	88
Clarinet	71	Cycle	29	Duster	73
Clay	72	Cycling	74		
Clean	12	Cygnet	39	**E**	
Clock	56, 57	Cymbal	71	Eagle	2, 33
Close	13	Cyr Wheel	86	Ear	44
Clothes	76			Earring	79
Clown	86	**D**		Earthworm	88
Clown's Bow	87	Daffodil	66	Easel	73
Clown's Cap	87	Dahlia	67	Eating	62
Clownfish	41	Daisy	66	Eel	40
Cluster Beans	24	Dancing	62	Eggplant	23
Cockroach	42	Deer	37	Eggs	11, 15
Coconut	20	Desk Calendar	73	Eighteen	7
Coffee Machine	60	Desk	73	Elbow	43
Cold	12	Dhol	69	Electrician	26
Colours	8, 72	Dholak	70	Elephant Calf	39

Elephant	9, 37	Fountain	84	Grilling Machine	61
Eleven	7	Four	6	Guava	19
Empty	12	Fourteen	7	Guinea Pig	34
Eraser	72	Fox	36	Guitar	69
E-Rikshaw	30	French Horn	70	Gun	48
Excited	46	Frock	76		
Exhaust Fan	59	Front	13	**H**	
Eye	44	Fruit Salad	15	Hair Band	79
Eyebrow	44	Fruits	16	Hair Brush	59
Eyelashes	44	Frying Pan	61	Hair Clips	79
Eyelid	44	Full	12	Hair Dryer	58
				Hair Oil	59
F		**G**		Hair	44
Face	43	Garbage Truck	29	Hairbrush	54
Face Painting	87	Garden Fork	89	Hamster	35
Fan	57	Garden Hose	88	Hanging Light	56
Farmer	26	Garden	88	Happy	13
Fast	12	Gardener	26	Hard	13
Fawn	38	Gas Lighter	61	Hare	37
Feeling Sad	63	Gas Stove	61, 82	Harmonica	70
Feet	43	Ginger	25	Harmonium	68
Fence	85	Giraffe	3, 36	Harp	69
Ferry	30	Glass	61	Hatchling	38
Fifteen	7	Globe	73	Head	43
Finger Puppets	50	Gloves	76	Hear	47
Finger	45	Glue	73	Heart	10
Fire Truck	29, 51	Go Cart	29	Heavy	12
Firefighter	27	Goat	34	Heel	43
Fireplace	56	Gold Ring	9	Helicopter	31
First Aid Kit	82	Golden	9	Hen	33, 34
Fish	15	Goldenberry	21	Hibiscus	66
Fishing Boat	31	Goldfish	34	Hiding	62
Five	6	Golf Cart	28	High Chair	52
Flamingo	33	Golf	74	Highlighter	72
Flask	83	Gong	69	Hiking Boots	82
Flower Bed	85	Goose	33, 34	Hippo	37
Flowerpot	56	Gooseberry	21	Honey	16
Flowers	2, 66	Gorilla	36	Honeycomb	88
Flute	70	Gown	76	Horse Racing	75
Foal	39	Grapes	18	Horse	35
Food	14, 55	Grass	88	Hospital	80
Food Wagon	28	Green Chilli	25	Hot Air Balloon	30
Football	11	Green House	88	Hot	12
Forearm	45	Green	8	Hotdog	14
Forehead	44	Grey	9	House	3

Hulk	48	Kitten	39	Magician	87
Hyena	37	Kiwi	18	Mandolin	71
		Knee	43	Mango	4, 19
I		Knife	61	Map	83
Ice Candy	9	Knuckle	45	Maracas	68
Ice Cream Cone	10	Koala	36	Marigold	67
Ice Cream	14	Kohlrabi	25	Marker	73
Ice	3			Mask	80
Insects	42	**L**		Mayo Tray	80
Inside	13	Labyrinth	49	Medical Gloves	80
		Lady Finger	22	Medicine	81
J		Ladybug	3, 42, 89	Merry-Go-Round	84
Jacket	77	Lamb	39	Microwave	61
Jackfruit	24	Lamp Post	84	Milk	14
Jar	61	Lamp	73	Mini Truck	31
Jasmine	67	Lantern	83	Mirror	11, 59
Java Plum	20	Laugh	63	Mittens	53
Jeans	77	Laughing	46	Mixer Grinder	60
Jeep	31, 50	Laundry Hamper	58	Monkey Bars	85
Jellyfish	41	Lavender	66	Monkey	36
Jet Ski	30	Leaf	10	Moon	10
Jet	31	Leaves	89	Morning Glory	66
Joey	38	Leg	43	Mosquito Net	54
Juggling	87	Light	12	Mosquito	42
Juice	3	Lighter	82	Motorcycle	28
Jujube	21	Lily	67	Mouth Freshener	58
Jumping Castle	51	Lion Cub	38	Muffin	15
Jumping	62	Lion	36	Mug	58
Jungle Gym	85	Lip	44	Mushroom	25
		Liquid	12	Musical Instruments	68
K		Listening	63	Muskmelon	20
Kangaroo	37	Litchi	19	My Body	43
Karate	74	Living Room	56	My Face	44
Kayak	31	Llama	35	My Hands	45
Kettle	3	Lobster	40	My Senses	47
Key Chain	78	Long Coat	76		
Keyboard	69	Loofah	58	**N**	
Kicking	65	Lorry	28	Nail	45
Kid	38	Lotus	66	Naseberry	19
Kingfisher	33	Luffa Gourd	23	Necklace	78
Kit	39	Lute	70	Nest	88
Kitchen Appliances	60			New	12
Kitchen Set	50	**M**		Nightgown	77
Kitchen	60	Magenta	9	Nightingale	32
Kite	10	Maggots	42	Nine	6

Nineteen	7	Path	84	Popcorn	16
Noodles	4, 17	Patient Walker	81	Poppy	66
Nose	44	Patient	81	Porcupine	37
Nostril	44	Praying	62	Postman	27
Notebook	73	Peas	23	Potato Chips	17
Notice Board	73	Peach	18	Potato Finger	16
Numbers	6	Peacock	32	Potato	24
Nurse	26, 81	Pear	21	Potty Seat	54
		Pen Corrector	72	Powder	55

O

		Pen Holder	72	Pram	53
Octopus	41	Pen	72	Pressure Cooker	60
Oil	52	Pencil	73	Pulling	63
Oil Tanker	29	Penguin	32	Pumpkin	22
Old	12	People at Work	26	Pupil	44
Omelette	17	Periwinkle	66	Puppy	4, 38
One	6	Pet & Farm Animals	34	Purple	9
Onion	22	Petunia	66	Purse	8
Open	13	Phone	51, 56	Push Chair	84
Opposites	12	Photographer	26	Pushing	63
Orange	4, 8, 19, 66	Piano	50, 69		

Q

Ostrich	32	Pick	63		
Otter	40	Picnic Basket	84	Question	4
Outside	13	Pig	35	Quilt	57
Oval	11	Pigeon	32		
Overalls	77	Piglet	39		

R

Owl	33	Pillow	53, 57	Rabbit	4, 35
Owlet	39	Pilot	26	Raincoat	77
Oyster	41	Pineapple	18	Rake	89
		Pink	8	Raspberry	21

P

		Pizza Slice	11	Rattle	51, 52
Pacifier	52	Pizza	14	Reading	63
Paint Palette	72	Plaster	81	Recorder	71
Painter	27	Plate	61	Rectangle	11
Painting	72	Play House	84	Red Chilli	24
Pajamas	76	Play Mat	55	Red	8
Palm	45	Playing	62	Refrigerator	60
Panda	36	Plum	19	Remote Car	49
Pansy	67	Plumber	27	Reporter	27
Papaya	19	Pointed Gourd	23	Rhinoceros	36
Paper	72	Polar Bear Cub	38	Rice	17
Parachute	31	Polar Bear	37	Ring Donut	48
Park Gate	85	Police Bike	50	Ring Master	87
Park	84	Police Car	51	Ring	79
Parrot	32, 35	Police Officer	26	Robin	33
Pasta	17	Pomegranate	19	Robot	48

Rocket	30, 48	Shells	41	Spin Rattle	49
Rocking Horse	51	Ship	31	Spinach	23
Roller Skates	85	Shirt	76	Spinning Top	10
Rolling Pin	61	Shoes	5	Sponge	58
Romper	52	Shorts	76	Spoon	53
Rooster	35	Shoulder	43	Sports	74
Rope Trapeze	86	Shower	59	Sprinkle	89
Rose	8, 66	Shrimp	15, 40	Square	11
Rubik's Cube	48	Singing	64	Squid	41
Rugby	75	Sipper	55	Stand	12
Ruler	73	Sit	12	Star Fruit	21
Running	65	Sitar	69	Star	10
		Six	6	Starfish	10, 40
S		Sixteen	7	Static Trapeze	86
Sad	13, 46	Skateboard	28	Statue	84
Salad	16	Skiing	74	Stethoscope	80
Sandpit	84	Skipping Rope	49	Sticking Plaster	81
Sandwich	11, 14	Skirt	76	Sticks	89
Sapphire	9	Sleeping Bag	82	Stingray	40
Sausage	17	Sleeping	64	Stomach	43
Saxophone	68	Sleepy	46	Strawberry	18
Scarf	76	Slide Car	49	Stretcher	81
School Bag	73	Slide	85	Stroller	53
School Bus	49	Slider	50	Submarine	31
School	72	Slow	12	Suit	77
Scientist	26	Small	13	Sunflower	8, 67
Scoop Stretcher	81	Smart Phone	48	Sunglasses	78
Scooter	28	Smell	47	Superman	48
Scorpion	42	Smiling	46	Surprised	46, 65
Sea Aeroplane	31	Snowmobile	28	Swan	33
Sea Animals	40	Soap Dish	58	Sweater	76
Sea Horse	40	Soap	55, 59	Sweatshirt	77
Sea Turtle	40	Soccer	74	Sweeping	65
Sea Urchin	40	Socks	54, 77	Sweet	13
Seal	40	Sofa	56	Swing	85
See Saw	84	Soft	13	Syringe	81
See	47	Soldier	27	Syrup	80
Seeds	89	Solid	12		
Seven	6	Soup	16	**T**	
Seventeen	7	Sour	13	Tabla	70
Shampoo	59	Spade	88	Table Lamp	57
Shapes	10	Sparrow	32	Table Tennis	74
Shark	41	Spatula	61	Tack	73
Shawl	76	Spider	42	Tadpole	39
Sheep	34	Spiderman	49	Talk	65

Tambourine	71	Tray	61, 81	Water Can	89
Tandem	28	Tree	84, 89	Water Lily	67
Taste	47	Triangle	11	Watermelon	19
Taxi	29	Trolley	51	Weight Lifting	75
Teacher	27	Trombone	69	Whale	41
Teddy	48	Trowel	89	Wheelbarrow	89
Teeth	44	Truck	29, 48	Wheelchair	80
Teether	55	Trumpet	71	Whisk	60
Television	11, 56	T-Shirt	77	Wild Animals	36
Ten	6	Tuba	68	Wolf	37
Tennis	75	Tulip	66	Woodpecker	32
Thermometer	81	Turnip	22	Woollen Cap	76
Thigh	43	Turtle	35	Wrist	45
Think	64	Twelve	7	Writing	64
Thinking	46	Twenty	7		
Thirteen	7	Two	6	**X**	
Three	6			Xylophone	5, 71
Throw	64	**U**			
Thumb	45	Unicycle	28	**Y**	
Tie	77	Up	13	Yacht	30
Tiger Cub	38	Utensils	5	Yak	35
Tiger	5, 37			Yawning	46
Tissue Paper	59	**V**		Yellow	8
Toaster	60	Van	29	Yogurt	14
Toe	43	Vegetables	22	Yolk	5
Toilet Paper	59	Video Camera	83		
Toilet Pot	58	Violin	68	**Z**	
Tomato	25	Volcano	5	Zebra	5, 37
Tongue	44	Volleyball	75		
Toothbrush	53, 58	Vulture	33		
Toothpaste	59				
Top	49	**W**			
Torch	47, 83	Walk	64		
Tow Truck	29	Walker	55, 81		
Towel	59	Walking Stick	80		
Toy Cycle	49	Wallet	78		
Toy Train	51	Walnut	5		
Toy	54	Walrus	40		
Toys	48	Wardrobe	57		
Tractor	29	Wash	65		
Traffic Cone	8	Washbasin	58, 60, 73		
Train	30	Washing Machine	59		
Tram	30	Washing Powder	58		
Transport	28	Watch	78		
Trapeze	86	Water Bottle	82		

www.ingramcontent.com/pod-product-compliance
Lightning Source LLC
Chambersburg PA
CBHW061058170426
43198CB00025B/2988